CONNECTED POETRY

Lizy J Campbell

2022

A series of free form poetry intertwined
together like fibers of a garment to create these
gentle present mindful connections.

The Connected Poetry book by Lizy J Campbell

Copyright 2022

Published by The Elite Lizzard Publishing Company 2022

Photo credit by: Te Rau Kendrick, gave me permission to use this gorgeous photo taken in Hawke's Bay area.

BREATHE

I hold my breath in
Centering
Remembering
The value of this inhale
I breathe
Out through the mouth I exhale
Letting the tension ease
Letting my muscles relax
Letting go of thoughts
Not picking up one
Let it work its course
Disappear
I inhale once more, slower, deeper still
From base of my spine to the tip of my head
Filling my lungs with love instead
In time and in practice my fears subside
I feel whole; I need not try
Eyes closed
Pay attention to the life-giving breath
A gift won't soon forget
Just breathe

FORGIVENESS

When dusk comes, the sun sinks and night looms
Nothing left of the day but to reflect

In darkness our transgressions we lay it to rest

Rejuvenating the mind in slumber

Dreaming of the new day to come

Putting faith on better

A new day with no mistakes

Loving and forgiving ourselves for things we
could not see

Forgiving those who hurt us the most

Realizing that love is sometimes blinding

CONNECTED

Stones and sand intermingled as one

The blue waves meet the streamlined skyline

Connecting earth and sky

Watching the tiny sea life moving with the tide

A wonderful thing to be alive

To be part of the cycle of life

A wondrous world full of creatures great and small

An interconnected tapestry of vibrational

beings

Forever moving in space and time

VOICE

Lost in speech
Like being in another world
A most conversational tune with natural flow

Enraptures the mind and intrigues the soul

A symphony of harmonious tones

All those who seek to listen

The heart knows the sounds of love

Building and becoming intertwined

Blind

The soft voice of a lover

owL

The glowing eyes of the

all-knowing owl perched
upon an old oak tree

Gazing over the night sky

Silently she lifts off glides through the darkness

The moon guiding her wings as she soars

She hunts her prey

Wise is she in the forest deep

The majestic life of an owl seeks to sleep

To hunt again in moonlit skies

CITY JUNGLE (COVID)

The city sleeps in this concrete cemetery

Cut off yet still full of life amongst homes

Keeping faith that this too will become a
distant memory
Holding on to one another

Families hold close

Realizing what truly matters

Things cannot be bought, statuses or power

Only found within the jungles deep

Is love

THE CAT

The Yellow cat's eyes peered out from the deep
forest stream

Its stillness of the water near reflected like two
stars

Gently it walks out of the dark to take in the

surroundings

The soft sounds of night perk her delicate ears as
she descends into the blackened night

All her senses heightened in the quiet
slight movements afar

Chasing prey in her elegant, elongated body as
she runs

Free as the wind with no attachments

The cat is ruler to no one

SOUL REPAIR

When looking into your eyes I see a thousand truths, a million lifetimes

Our past the shadows it hides

Knowingly accepting and working hard to cast away old ties

Building a new view

Healing from the inside out

Casting out shadows of doubt

Healing traumas and wounds

A lesson of a twin flame

Level up

FALL

The colored leaves sprinkle the forest floor

The crisp wind dances with the leaves

Swirling about as they play

The atmosphere mesmerizing

The trees just sway

This hypnotic dance

Put in a trance

A beauty of letting go

Nothing ever stays the same

We are forced in life to play the game

Knowing that things will never be again

Life's view through a season

Cycle of being human

BLUE SKIES

The sky so clear, so unscathed

The beauty in looking up to view blue

A reminder when clouds cover over

That darkness in skies never stay forever

We just need to hold on a little longer

Nothing lasts and nothing stays

We will see those sunny days

Brave those gray days

Grateful the blue sky is always above

SPACE

Galaxies unknown,

A vast space amongst the stars

Stars older than time, lights the night skyline

A wondrous place for the imagination

A playground for minds to roam

In deep thought creators write

Adventures of things never sought

Other worlds an exploration

What a wonderful place is the space in the mind
for such imagination

GREEN

The rain-soaked clouds filled and ready to burst

To bring life to earth

To awaken deep roots

To refresh, nourish, and cleanse

Lush green gardens bloom life and die

Recycled into the earth

Its cycle gives the soil a new life

WILD DESIRE

The watchful eye hidden in plain view

A gleaming eye spots its trinkets

Silence as it attacks

Fangs dig deeply into its prey

A primal need

Unlike humans' desires

Craving and giving in

Humans in a wild concrete jungle of sin

GUARDIAN ANGEL

Feathers of an angel hold my soul in refuge

A guide in protection, in thoughts and in life

An invisible force, a warrior of humanity

A stoic but powerful presence

Beautiful yet silent

The angel shows signs and little hints

to those who watch

It protects me from harm of things I know not

Grateful I am guided through life

Within the arms of my guardian angel

LIQUID MINDFULNESS

Warm liquid flows down my throat

It warms my soul

Its dark golden liquid touches my lips, bliss

These beautiful tea leaves, from fields of flowers
it grows

Hot water pours and the smell kisses my nose

I sit and am reminded mindfully as I taste

Remembering this moment right now

The moment that counts

SEA THERAPY

My head breaks the surface of the water

Water wraps around me engulfed like a blanket

Bright waves move by the illuminated sun
speckled waters

I just float

Water rejuvenates my soul

Lost in this state of restfulness

Natures natural healing place

MOUNTAINS

The snowy peak glistens in the mountainous
atmosphere

The uppermost snow a blindingly bright white in
the sun

The birds fly high above the mountains

Their calls echo in the silence of the snows

insulation

A frozen preserved piece of time

A majestically still presence

A monumentally impressive work of art

In the dead of winter

REBIRTH

Engulfed by life's past

These green vines interconnect and entangle

Man's historical buildings it breaks down into
rubble

It weaves through cracks and crevices

Vegetation the winner

An abandoned city no more

Taking back natures house

A silent rebirth

DREAMER

As I lay in this current place my thoughts start
to wander

Dreams of realms beyond,
where good times never cease

Raised hands to the skyline, I feel free

A breeze passing over me helps me breathe

I close my eyes, let it touch my skin

A perfect balance for my inner world to begin

My mindset at play

Cast away from the troubles of the day

I create my new future

My new happy ending

Dreaming it into my reality

THE WRITER

I felt naked from the words inscribed in my head, down to the most intimate of places

Shed my exoskeleton of past tense, vulnerable yet curiously beckoning me

Brightly lit words drip from lips as silken honey, reveals deepening bonds

Organically meshed and beautifully crafted, like orchestrated music

Writing things into existence that held my thoughts

No boundaries

The pen and paper, my oyster

WIND

The winds of change I couldn't predict

This journey to another land, someplace greener
or maybe someplace grand

The excitement of the unplanned is all part of
exploring the new

Let the wind take me as the wind builds up

Whichever way it moves me, I will just go

Trusting that its not for me to know the how or
why

Its just up to me to learn to trust that I will fly
when its time

RIVER

The rivers surface shimmers like jewels

Hearing the water turning over sounds hypnotic

I contemplate a lifetime of extraordinary people
who stood by me

Who helped me keep flowing just as the river
drives the fish down stream

Ever changing cycles we too are part of nature

Our body an invisible force of love for life

The time passes and great lessons learned

This river of life we canoe through

To paddle upstream makes no sense

Go with life's flow with confidence

SNAKE

The snake slithers across the soil without a sound

It takes it victim by surprise

Eating it whole without a trace

Sneaks and moves about with such precision

Shedding its skin, it becomes renewed

Growing long wrapped in trees like tangled yarn

It blends in where ever it roams

A methodical predator

The snake

LOST

Her mood infectious, a stormy sea

It rocked foundations and caused enormous uncertainty

A castaway with no clear destination, gazing off into the blackest skies

A drift, forever searching

Soul searching and self-healing, continuously changing as the churning sea

Lost in the sea of so many lies

The sea, him it swallowed her whole

Drowned in sorrow

She reached out her hand and broke through

Pulled out and saved

The ship of faith

DISCOVERY

The words flow from his lips

Unsuspectingly it caresses my body

He fingered the deepest desires of my mind

Sweet nothings and soft whispers of lies he tells

He is bearing rotten fruit as his heartbeat pulses
faster knowing he's tricked

Just a while longer as the game continues

Eyes covered in the depths of this chatter

A treasure found to be false

A discovery of truths

SUMMER

The strawberries I taste remind me of hot
summer days, cool lemonades
and wearing shades

The sweetness of nature's gifts

Sun-kissed skin glistens with lotion

Losing ourselves to the shade of a willow tree

Its shadow dances upon the pages of a summer
read

Oh, how I love that warmth on my skin

Feeling the sand shifting tickling my toes

I will treasure it always

Summer days

WHITE NOISE

Looking for a white noise

A distraction

A monumental alteration to thinking about
thinking

The diagnosis, a musical intervention

Music to keep my mind at bay

To disturb the thought cells encased within

Beautiful distraction of rhythm

I happily let my ears infuse me to a higher
vibration

Let the noise disturb my thoughts

Closing my eyes

Just feel the rhythm

NATURE

The gentle cool breeze on my skin moves the peach hair on my arm

Caressing my nerve endings, sending welcome chills down my spine

Dried up all my tears

It's everywhere I look if I choose to see

Nature's beauty

BUBBLE POP

Happy bubbles float along lifting off with its
iridescent rainbow of hollow spheres

Its life is short but brings many smiles

Creating a whimsy for a beautiful atmospheric
delight for the brains fantasy

And Pop!

The structure bursts spontaneously

A great entertainment and joy

Something so small and so insignificant

But large in happiness

KIND

Even though there are billions of stars in the
sky

The one I search for is brighter than the rest

It never fades or loses its sparkle

When my eyes find it my soul knows

It cradles out in its ethereal glow

Carrying out kindness despite hurts

Capable of being seen but never a show

I can see its true beauty

Its love forever instilled

Kind people just glow

FIREFLY

A lonely firefly danced on the edge of the pond

It twirled and pivoted at the vastness of space

Realized not her essence of beauty

Lucky for the moments that match the scenery

A firefly lights up the night sky

Like stars from heaven it glows here on earth

Not knowing just how magnificent

It brings joy to those who can capture a glimpse

A glow of pure innocence

WORDS

I write to soothe my craving soul in fits of hunger
for words

Words that need to express

The inner workings and intricate thoughts of a
mind that never rests

Ambition moves mountains

Even more when stones are thrown

When life's challenges bend realities and seem
to distort the goal

But only for a moment

It is in those darkened moments inspiration
flows, just like a river

It is connected to my soul

PEACE

The sun shone as it danced upon the dew like diamonds

The clouds moved to a waltzing dance only it knew

Birds flew and filled the sky with life as time stopped to embrace their beauty

An enchanted amber sky emerges as the sun moves on beyond the horizon

Bringing peace and tranquility with it

Watching its fleeting beauty I am filled with peace

LEAF

Hold me up to the sun
Look through me

Veins and little imperfections
Specs of a different color

The texture I feel between fingers
Run it along the ridges

It amazes me how beautiful something can be
The stem sturdy, letting go at just the right time

The color so vibrant

The leaf it's just one but shows strength
Health and vitality of a tree's life

Individually its weak but together strong
Each feeding the roots to keep

Its mindful to stop and take a break
To break down what we forget to see
To appreciate all the wonders life
To remember that we are all part of this great
synergy

VIBES

Do I know you?
We have never met before

I can sense there is more to you then I see with eyes

Something about that energy
The way you speak seems to go right through me

My soul listened with great care
The vibe picked up

That something wasn't adding up
Forgetting to trust the gut

We ignore because we don't want to believe

That hate to a vibration

Our body sends the alarm

Heed the call and keep your guard
Protect your energy

Your sign is soft but it's there
Vibes don't lie

THANK YOU FOR READING THIS SHORT POETRY BOOK ABOUT LIFE AND NATURE!

If you liked these poems, I have three more emotionally charged poetry books available online.

You can find all my books worldwide online under <u>Lizy J Campbell</u>

Lizy J Campbell Born in Toronto,ON Canada. She is an ambitious multi-genre author, illustrator, and publishing company business owner.
She has over 24 books published since 2018.

www.ingramcontent.com/pod-product-compliance
Lightning Source LLC
Chambersburg PA
CBHW070955120626
46546CB00004B/1631